A BEGINNER'S GUIDE TO MAGIC MUSHROOMS

ALEX GIBBONS

UPDATES

For a chance to go into the draw to win a FREE book every month like our 'Stoner Themed Coloring Book' (below), and other updates on our latest books, subscribe below!

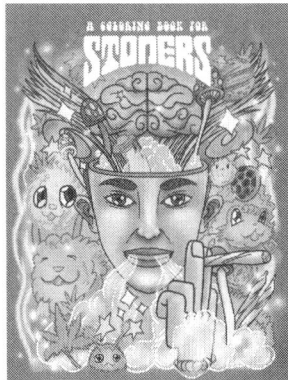

https://psychedeliccuriosity.activehosted.com/f/1

For daily posts on all things Psychedelic, follow us on Instagram @Psychedelic.curiosity

Mushrooms can heal, feed and possibly enlighten you - maybe even help save the world.

— DR. PAUL STAMETS

CONTENTS

1

INTRODUCTION

Nature's psychedelic truffles, magic mushrooms, have been part of human cultures for thousands of years. From the Sahara to Guatemala, they have always provided human beings with a natural means to get high. What's more, they have been part of arts and culture, as well as academic interest, and have held great ritual and spiritual importance in cultures across the globe.

'Shrooms', or magic mushrooms, are what we call the fungi that have hallucinogenic properties called psilocybin. They are naturally growing psychedelic drugs with a long history and an intertwined relationship with human cultures across the globe. They produce mind-altering effects and cause hallucinations, out-of-the-ordinary thought patterns and hypnotic and trance-like states. The experiences encountered on magic mushrooms are generally called a 'trip.'

They grow in the wild in woodlands, grasslands and plains and are fairly universal in their distribution. They can also be cultivated artificially but they are illegal in many countries. The fascinating thing is, they have long been taken for recreational use, healing functions and in spiritual and creative endeavors. They were rediscovered in the west in the 1950s, and remain one of the most popular hallucinogens in under 35s in the United States according to some reports.

We have written this beginner's guide to take you on a journey through the fun, the facts, the science, the dangers and the benefits of magic mushrooms. While reading this won't qualify you as a *mycologist* - a mushroom expert - or instantly make you a mushroom guru like Stamet - a world-leading mycologist - it will offer you everything you need to know to begin your journey of discovery about magic mushrooms, types, history, culture, dosage, trips (historical and modern day), side effects, dangers, scientific research, and much more. While we don't advocate their use, growth or illegal activity in any way, we are offering you everything we know and have found about magic mushrooms in order for you to remain aware.

Through this explorer's guide, you will see through case reports, or 'trip' reports, academic research and historical records of magic mushrooms on cave paintings. These mystical little fungi have sparked emotions and experiences as diverse as the spectrum of the entire universe. From euphoria, visual alterations, right through to creative impulses, paranoia or anxiety, they have played a significant role in the human experience throughout time and across space.

Beginning our guide, you can go on a journey through time and space through the prism of magic mushrooms in the section about history and culture.

We then explore the most common types of magic mushrooms, and look at their active properties. This section describes the physical features of the two most common types and how to identify them, as well as the dangers of picking magic mushrooms. We explore some little-known stories and look at the first ever trip report from 1799, and the first viral trip report from 1955 that let a huge mushroom-shaped, Mexican secret, out of the bag for good.

We then shift a gear to look at the recreational use of magic mushrooms. If you are interested in the ways people get hold of magic mushrooms, or grow them, you can explore those themes and also look at dosages, the longevity and preparation of magic mushrooms, and how they are ingested.

Do you want to know what it is like to experience magic mushrooms without taking them? Don't take your friends' word for it, or look at the mystical depictions in films. We avoid glamourising mushrooms and give you an array of real-life experiences from real life trip reports; the next best thing to experiencing them yourself. We summarise three experiences found by journalers online which all give genuine insights into the inner world of magic mushrooms from different perspectives. These are the good, the bad, the ugly, and everything in between. Get a clearer picture of the array of emotions that happen while on a magical mushroom journey. What's more, these experiences are all backed by cases within scientific research. You may even begin to see patterns emerging; psychedelic ones.

We outline the dangers of magic mushrooms and point out what is going on at a chemical level in the brain too. Following this, we offer up a few findings from recent studies on psychedelic therapies and the potential for possible benefits to mental health disorders outlined by a few scholars.

If you want a quick fact sheet, we provide a FAQs section at the end; a speedy glance at everything you might need to know about magic mushrooms, simply put. As a bonus, we give you some quick-fire do's and don'ts. As with everything in this guide, as we tell you in the legalities section, mushrooms are illegal. We just want you to have the facts and know what to do to keep as safe as possible, or stop you or your tripping friends from going into a hole.

So, sit back, relax, and enjoy this explorer's guide…

2

HISTORY

Magic mushrooms came back to Europe in the 1950s when a *mycologist* called Wisson traveled through Mexico to study them. A huge stir came about; this man published his findings in *Life* magazine, and people began to flock to the drug. There was an outcry from governments, and these were just the thing young hippies had been looking for to make a break from the previous generation. This article is in no small part one of the things that sparked the psychedelic era: a wave of popular culture and a whole movement was fuelled somewhat by the recreational use of magic mushrooms. What most people don't know, however, is that 'shrooms' date back to way before, into ancient times. People were recording trip reports before the invention of writing.

Deep into the caves of the baking hot Sahara desert, there are depictions of magic mushrooms that have been dated to 9000 BC in what is now Algeria. Early hunter-gatherers painted on cave walls, leaving us a record of their experiences of magic mushrooms. Historians are convinced these are *Psilocybe Mairei*, a local mushroom of the area. It seems the properties of mushrooms in opening up different avenues of the mind have meant they were used in spiritual contexts. Who knows, some of these experiences may have been profound, godly and spiritual, and some may have led to introspective staring at the infinite grains of sand on the desert! We can imagine that humans have always experienced the natural psychoactive properties of mushrooms in ways that are unique to them as a person, yet profoundly human and universal.

And in Europe? Spotted in Spain, there was a real buzz some years ago when a research team discovered 6000-year-old rock art on a cave mural. The Selva Pascuala mural is just outside the town of Villar del Humo and is the oldest evidence of their use in Europe.

This painting mainly depicts a bull but also interestingly shows thirteen small little capped mushrooms along the bottom of the painting. Due to their long, fine, stems, varying between straight and curvy, and their small dome-like caps, just like the real thing, the famous expert in Psilocybe, Gaston Guzman, confirmed that these are local versions of the mushrooms with hallucinogenic properties called *Psilocybe hispanica*.[1]

It is likely, therefore, these were used to open up new perspectives and cognitive experiences, perhaps during religious rituals, or even during artistic expression itself.

The spiritual

While their use may have oscillated between recreational and spiritual over time, the transcendent properties endowed to humans by mushrooms mean that they have often been utilized in ceremonial practices, shamanic rituals and by spirit mediums, as well as those on a more personal spiritual journey.

Where these cave paintings occurred in areas that mushrooms grow, there is some artistic proof that hallucinogenic mushrooms were used in controlled ritual practices with numerous dimensions and strands. On these rock paintings were portrayals of god-like figures wearing masks and adorned with mushrooms, where ritual offerings were made.

Coupled with evidence from other parts of the world, it is thought that magic mushrooms were taken with great ritual importance, in events of mystic-religious practices. Ancient Mayan and Aztec peoples were thought to use magic mushrooms to produce trance-like states, communicate with gods, and create visions.[2] Not much unlike modern-day experiences, as you can check out in the trip reports and recorded stories later in this guide.

The psyche

Shrooms spiraling out of human heads, tripping, painting and describing. These depictions were left in the far reaches of the Artic many years ago. While this was way before sharing and 'going viral', depictions of *the effects* of magic mushrooms were left in another old-school record. Scholar, Dikov, discovered the Pegtymel petroglyph 40 miles (60 kilometers) from the Arctic on the Pegtymel River, with funky pictures of people with mushrooms coming out of their heads, reminiscent of psychedelic art.[3]

Could these be an early artist's way of showing the effects that mushrooms have on the human psyche? This particular strain was thought to be *Amanita* Mushrooms, or *Amanita Muscaria*, ingested by the Chukchi people.

A creative impulse

One thread running through this guide, and it seems over time, is the creative impulse that comes about through magic mushrooms. Just like in the psychedelic sixties there is an idea that hallucinogens have provided inspiration for artistic depictions themselves, or that these early artists were under the influence of magic mushrooms.

Lewis-Williams and Dowson, in 1988, put forward that there are many cave depictions or petroglyphs that were painted under the influence of mind-altering natural produce. European petroglyphs are covered in non-literal images and patterns such as lines, zigzags and circles, all thought to be potentially produced when in a mind-altered state.

This creative buzz is something that can be carried through to the psychedelic era right into the modern day. We will see a bit of this creative impulse further on in trip report one, a doodler from the U.S. who documents his experiences in drawings and writings.

Mushrooms in the psychedelic sixties: Psychedelic art and music

In Europe and the States, throughout the psychedelic sixties and seventies, mushrooms took people on new spiritual journeys that became characteristic of the era, along with their synthetic friend, LSD, or acid. Psychedelia characterized the day and made up a whole subculture that would carry on through decades of music, art and popular influence.

Like the thought process while on magic mushrooms, this art was hypnotic, varied in patterns and mystical. Bright colors and dissonant, deep, distorted, trippy, sounds, permeated the human psyche, where youth movements, free-living and a move towards open-mindedness provided a counter-culture to the backdrop of the post-war decades. Think late Beatles, think sitar, think Sergeant Pepper's.

Once more, experiences on mind-altering drugs were depicted in art, which used vibrant colors, non-representational forms, shapes and spectrums to try to recreate the experiences encountered whilst tripping. This art and music not only artistically reflects the tripping journey, it was created to be enjoyed whilst experiencing the effects of mushrooms themselves.

Our next section takes a little look at what magic mushrooms are, and the facts. We do go into some more early experiences in this section, before looking at the recreational side of the drugs and trip reports.

3

WHAT'S IN A 'SHROOM'? THE FACTS

These natural growing hallucinogens have played a part in culture at various moments in history, but what exactly are they? And what is in them to induce some of the feelings we have talked about already?

What are magic mushrooms?

Magic mushrooms are small fungal species that contain the properties that trigger certain neurochemical responses in the brain. There are hundreds upon hundreds of types of psilocybin-containing species growing all over the world. We might call them magic little fungal globetrotters.

So, what's in them?

The hallucinogenic substances within the mushroom are psilocybin, psilocin and baeocystin, known to induce various effects on the human brain, such as euphoria, altered consciousness, dissolving of the ego (sense-of-self), altered behavior and concentration span, anxiety and paranoia. In fact, there is a whole array of responses and magic mushroom experiences that depend on the person, the environment, and the dose.

Neurochemical effects: what it does to the brain

Scientists have a pretty good idea about the chemical ways mushrooms affect the brain. Psilocybin binds to the 5-HT2A receptor, the serotonin receptor in the brain, thus sparking a wave of electrochemical signals.[4]

The chemical makeup of psilocybin, psilocin and serotonin are actually pretty similar, as represented in the following visual (figure 1). Psilocin hence attaches itself to serotonin, which is the brain's chemical way of making us happy.

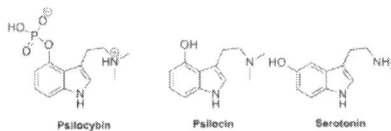

Psilocybin   Psilocin   Serotonin

Figure 1. The structures of the main components of Psilocybe, psilocybin and psilocin, show marked similarity with serotonin.

If you are listening to the audio see the attached pdf guide to look at the images.

The legality of magic mushrooms

The schedule 1 drugs psilocin and psilocybin mean that possession of the mushrooms containing them in the United States is illegal. Spores do not contain these substances but are nonetheless illegal in Georgia, Idaho and California. However, selling spores is illegal in all states, especially selling them for the purposes of growing hallucinogenic mushrooms: it is outlawed by the Louisiana State Act 1959.

There have been some moves to legalize magic mushrooms, by those jumping on the cannabis bandwagon. A few in Denver and Oregon, for example, are pushing for its decriminalization. They are using the potential scientific research into the controlled use of psychedelics in treating mental health disorders as their springboard for this action.

Interesting fact: mushrooms were legal in the UK until very recently. Until 2005, you could pop to your local market or head shop and buy them over the counter and at music festivals. 'Shroom' dealers could have business cards and display posters of the various types: 'Harry Potters' and 'Mexican Blues', displaying pictures on their walls. Oddly, they went straight from 'legal' to class A, the most serious category of illegal drugs (along with heroin and cocaine) in the UK. Rumour has it that they became illegal during a few music festivals in August, where mushroom vendors had to give them away after midnight when the law changed and they could no longer sell them.

What types are there?

There are way too many types of psilocybin mushrooms to list in total here, over 180. There are books dedicated to the topic. The foremost expert is Stamets, but our further reading section gives you some insight into the books available. That said, let's have a look at some common types, and a few bonus 'shrooms' thrown in there for your interest. Most of them have pretty long Latin names but, of course, as anyone who has bought mushrooms would tell you, they have a whole host of street names, strains and types too.

We'll start off with one of the most commonly known, Liberty Caps, or *Psilocybe Semilanceata*.

. . .

Liberty Caps

Figure 2. Fruit bodies of the hallucinogenic mushroom Psilocybe Semilanceata. Specimens photographed in Sweden.

This little shroom really packs a punch as one of the most potent around. It grows nearly everywhere there are wet grasslands: from the UK and Austria, to the Channel Islands, the Pacific Northwest and British Columbia. There are a few reports of its presence in the hill regions of Tamil Nadu in India. Figure 2 shows you Liberty Caps in *situ* in Sweden, quite innocent looking, right?

Five ways to identify Liberty Caps

While we strongly advise against picking your own mushrooms (in fact, this is the greatest danger attached to the drug and can result in death), there are 5 ways you can identify Liberty Caps for scientific purposes:

1. Firstly, think about where they are found and what type of

terrain (grassy wetlands in Europe and parts of North America and Canada).

2. Secondly, look at the cap of the mushroom itself to see if it is small and conical.
3. Number three sounds obvious, but observe carefully the color and the size and shape of the stem, which should be lighter than the brown cap, long and thin.
4. Next, check out the gills (the bits underneath the cap). You should see that the gills are narrowly attached and cream in color.
5. Final top tip: to be 100% sure, you can take a spore print by leaving it on a piece of paper for 2-6 hours. You can then look under a microscope.

Liberty Caps can be found growing in autumn mostly, before the first frosts, and normally in September. Seasoned 'shroomers' live for this picking season, and their annual trip to a known spot. As our legal section outlines, possession of any form of magic mushrooms is against the law in most countries. Not only that, they are very easily misidentified.

Liberty Caps have a pretty interesting case study from London we wanted to share with you. We could call this the first written trip report in history.

The first trip report in history: A family affair

So unlike other trip reports in this guide, this one was not found online. It wasn't your typical spiritual journey or even an expected trip to begin with. It happened in 1799 in London, with a man and his kids. This trip was a bit of a family affair and is one of the first modern documented uses of Liberty Caps and of mushrooms in Europe. [5]

Imagine this, you, your mum, and your dad, munch upon an innocent looking mushroom in the park before you all temporarily lose your minds, burst into fits of laughter and total and utter confusion, and watch each other's pupils dilate. This is what happened to a father of four in 1799 when he made a family meal with mushrooms picked in London's Green Park. This is not only an interesting bit of history, it gives you some insight into the effects of magic mushrooms. It also gives a 'family day trip' a whole new meaning.

Trip report disclaimers and warnings

This story could be one of those urban myths! It should be noted that in general, overcooking mushrooms takes away their psychoactive properties. So unless this guy made a mushroom salad, there could be some slight exaggeration involved here. Still, it is a 'charming' story, aside from the thought of child abuse! Obviously, it goes without saying that giving children any substances, illicit or otherwise, is completely and utterly abhorrent, even in 1799.

Since 1998, Liberty Caps come with a bit of an additional warning label too: there have been reports of traces of phenethylamine in them, which could cause adverse reactions. Scientists are not too sure about the exact amounts of the phenethylamine within them yet, but it is well worth noting that anything growing and illegal is unregulated and untested, and thus a bit of a lottery.

The next mushroom on our list has its roots in Mexico...

THE MEXICAN: PSILOCYBE CUBENSIS

Figure 3. Psilocybe Cubensis. Source: WikiCommons. Credit: Rohan523 (2009).

Another mushroom commonly found is the *Psilocybe Cubensis*. This one has a tall thick stalk in comparison to the Liberty Cap. The middle of the stem is a bright blue, indicating potent amounts of the substance psilocin. This gives them a pretty psychedelic appearance on the inside, despite their innocent looking exterior. The picture of the dried mushrooms in figure 4 shows their bluish tinge.

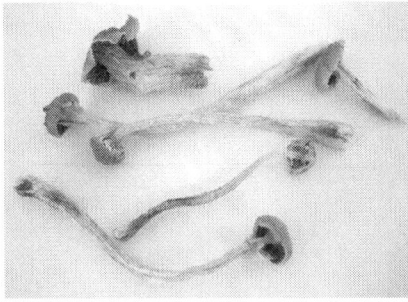

Figure 4. Dried Psilocybe Cubensis magic mushrooms. Source: wiki commons. Credit: Erik Fenderson (2006).

In the Netherlands, where there are some slightly more relaxed laws on magic mushrooms, this mushroom is called a Mexican mushroom because, you guessed it, this mushroom is largely found in Mexico. This psychedelic is an extremely popular natural psychedelic drug.

It is readily found as it is easy to grow. In Holland, while the mushroom itself is banned, you can by grow kits well within the limits of the law. Figure 5 shows these cubensis growing in a box at home and figure 6 shows the magnified spore print. Spore prints are a bit like the fingerprint of a mushroom, and each one has its own unique pattern when observed under a microscope.

Figure 5. Growbox with nearly mature p. Cubensis. Source: WikiCommons. Credit: LordToran

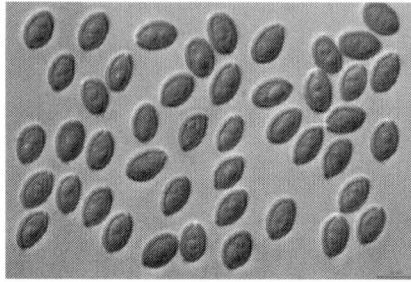

Figure 6. Psilocybe Cubensis spores, 1000 times magnification illuminated with DIC. Source: Wikicommons, Alan Rockefella (2013).

A 1950s trip report that went 'viral'

The Mexican secret of thousands of years was let out the bag by a curious American researcher in the 1950s. The Velada, Maria Sabina and the 'healing' Mexican mushroom became a smash hit around the world.

This Mexican mushroom was encountered by a mushroom expert through the ritual session of a certain Maria Sabina. The secret was let out the bag, causing a wave of trippers, both physically and metaphorically, to flock to the Mexican (the person and the mushroom).[6]

In Mexico, the *Psilocybe Cubensis* mushroom had been used in the Velada session for centuries. Maria Sabina used mushrooms to communicate with the gods and heal the sick in this ritualistic practice.

In the early 1950s, Wasson met the Mazatec curandera (medicine woman or healer) Maria Sabina, before eating mushrooms and recording them, sending a craze around the world for these psychedelic drugs. While this practice had largely been a secret for the rest of the world and carried out by experienced practitioners in Mexico, this was the start of recreational discovery. News of this mushroom went wild, and the *Psilocybe Cubensis* had more than its fifteen minutes of fame. Hippie tourists flocked to Maria's village for a hit, and the Mexican mushroom was used far and wide in the United States until it was banned in 1966. The banning of this mushroom in Mexico in 1970 saw the total end of this practice but not of the mushroom, which is still sold illegally, and grown. So, this 'trip report' wasn't shared online either but certainly had a monumental impact, introducing the world of mushrooms, tripping, and psychedelics, to a vast audience.[7]

Psilocybe azurescens, or 'Azzies'

These are reportedly the most potent of all mushrooms, containing massive amounts of psychoactive compounds that make you trip. It bruises blue, demonstrating the high levels of psilocin. This one also contains baeocystin and norbaeocystin and is reportedly capable of paralyzing your muscles.

It is found, but only by absolute experts (who keep their location secret) in the Pacific Northwest U.S. People have been known to buy the spores online and have encountered a few batches (probably through amateur growth outdoors). As usual, the mushroom guru, Stamets, reported its discovery back in 1995.

A highbrow trip report, from a professional writer

Writers do have a way with words, something that is equally useful and misleading at times. Michael Pollan paints a somewhat pretty picture of his experiences on 'azzies', which he picked with Stamets himself of all people. Not only did he write a compelling book, *How to Change Your Mind: What the New Science of Psychedelics Teaches Us About Consciousness, Dying, Addiction, Depression, and Transcendence,* he published an engaging extract online, in the Atlantic, no less.

He pitches some pretty interesting questions to academics about why, biologically, ecologically, and from an evolutionary perspective, mushrooms contain psychoactive properties. "Was it a defense mechanism to ward-off being eaten? And, how are the spores dispersed?", he asked. The answers lead to a mention of some pretty out-there animal trip reports. Horses getting high. Whatever next? His own, artsy, well-crafted, trip report is worth a read, but these mushrooms are probably best avoided by your average Joe.

5

THE RECREATIONAL USE OF MUSHROOMS

Aside from the facts, the history and the scientific info, we come right into the recreational use of mushrooms. If they are illegal, where do people get them? What do they do with them when they do? And how do they experience them?

Where do you get magic mushrooms?

While shrooms can be found growing in most countries around the world, most people avoid hunting and picking them themselves. Not least because possession of them is illegal in most countries because of the banned substances within them but, moreover, because there are so many varieties of mushrooms.

Even in a best-case scenario where you don't pick a toxic mushroom, you won't trip because picking a similar looking strain of the cousin you are after won't contain psilocybin. A slightly better (but not so brilliant) outcome of picking the wrong mushrooms would be a dodgy stomach, severe cramps or even hospitalization.

Most people will tell you, picking a mushroom with only a slightly different diameter cap could result in death. The big laughing gym, as it is commonly referred, will do a bit of both: it has psilocybin (probably not even enough to get you high) but is classed as poisonous, making you sick and ripping your stomach to shreds.

Although they are illegal in most countries, there is always a black market for them. Mushrooms are generally sold in the U.S. in eighths, meaning one-eighth of an ounce (3.5 grams), which usually costs around $20.

Picking them wild is an option for some but, as we made clear above, it's a risk you don't want to take as identifying mushrooms can be difficult. Some people grow them at home, most commonly grown being *Cubensis,* as they are reportedly the easiest to grow.

In the UK, although the active component Psilocybe is illegal, whether sold dried, fresh or prepared, head shops get around this law by selling spores in suspension under the guise of being for microscopy and microbiological purposes.

People buy them in the form of spore syringes, costing between ten and twenty dollars in the U.S. You can buy spore prints which have to be rehydrated before growing. Information on how to grow can also be found in various places online. Again, this can be extremely tricky. Failing to create the kind of sterile environment mushrooms need to grow could result in contamination. Contamination can result in either unsuccessful crops or, worse still, a batch that is bad for you.

How much do you take?

Dosage is a lottery with shrooms. Beginners are advised to start on a low dose (one gram) because of the unknown effects of the mushrooms but also the very variable potencies of mushrooms. It is always worth waiting an hour to see how you feel at that point, although the experience will change over the course of the trip. The way the mushrooms are prepared can also cause issues. Different strains also have different effects and are advised in varying amounts. Likewise, whether the mushrooms are dried or fresh affects the dosage. *Cubensis* comes in various forms and its Thai versions, for example, are thought to be way stronger and more intense than the supposedly more mellow versions from the Gulf Coast.

Psilocybin is one of the main active properties of magic mushrooms and to feel the effects of the drug, you have to take between three and thirty mg. There is a bit more detail in our FAQ. People vary their doses from micro-dosing, to strong doses of up to five grams. Your tolerance to mushrooms decreases over time so people can find themselves having to take more and more in order to feel the same effects.

Micro-dosing is something that is said to induce creativity, while you won't feel the strong effects of mushrooms. Increasing the dose up to one gram may alter your perceptions slightly but would normally not cause changes to vision and states that medium strong doses of three grams and strong doses of five grams would.

How do people take magic mushrooms?

Mushrooms can be eaten fresh or dried, brewed into mushroom tea, taken in pill or liquid form, or prepared into other drinks or food.

Eating them

While it is possible to eat them, mushrooms are reported to have a terrible taste; either bitter or floury and are sort of saliva-inducing in a bad way. Eating fresh can also induce stomach cramps.

People have been known to come up with some funky ways to disguise the taste. You could cook a chilli, maybe even a mushroom pizza or a smoothie. Alternatively, for those non-cooks, peanut butter, jam, or fruit is another alternative. Or, some just have a drink at hand to wash them down. However, cooking the mushrooms too much with too much heat will give a weaker effect and reduce the impact of the psychoactive ingredient, psilocybin.

. . .

Mushroom tea and other drinks

Another popular alternative is mushroom tea. Be under no illusions, this is not your normal brew and may not taste or look particularly pleasant either.

Many people prefer to make mushroom tea rather than eat them fresh, which can lessen the effect of stomach upset but also make you feel the effects much more quickly. Stomach cramps can be really distracting and unwelcoming, especially if you are tripping for the first time.

Mushrooms can be cut into smaller bits, or for smaller varieties, you can boil them whole and make 'shroom tea'. The way to make tea is to brew the mushrooms for twenty minutes in hot water, leaving the fresh mushrooms at the bottom. The mushroom liquid (which could be a brownish color) is then poured into cups, and whole mushrooms or pieces are added to the cups too. These pieces of mushrooms can still be eaten after drinking the liquid itself but they won't be as strong. Tea will make you feel the effects more quickly but you will come down quicker as well.

Some people soak mushrooms in alcohol, such as tequila, and combine the two substances. In our mixology section, however, we do advise against such mixing.

Mushroom pills

Mushrooms could be ground and packed into gelatine pills. The taste and texture can be avoided this way, but it would be difficult to see what was inside each pill. You would not actually know what you are getting.

Mushroom mixology: drugs to avoid on magic mushrooms

Like all substances, things can mix around in your body in mysterious ways. We go into some detail here about what to avoid whilst taking magic mushrooms.

Mushrooms are generally considered fairly safe in comparison to some drugs in terms of pharmaceutical risks, however, when mixing, it can sometimes have negative reactions.

- **Tramadol/Prozac**

Because magic mushrooms are a serotonin agonist, it is not generally advised to take mushrooms whilst on these drugs. You will read varying reports online but there is limited scientific research. People with issues with mental health are generally to steer clear of mushrooms and other non-prescription drugs.

- **Cocaine /Amphetamines**

This mix is generally agreed on through experience and through scientific reports. Coke, LSD and mushrooms do not mix well on a chemical level or in terms of psychological effects. Reports go from "overpowers the trip" to "uncomfortable and edgy" and many people agree that coming down on coke is not fun whilst on mushrooms. As one "seasoned tripper" put it, they are on different ends of the "trip spectrum."

- **Alcohol**

Generally, alcohol will just make you more out of your senses and you won't experience the mushrooms in the same way. You may not notice the negative side effects of one which is a plus however, the alcohol could potentially make you sick.

6

THE EXPERIENCE

Now we are getting into the experiences of magic mushrooms, looking first of all at how it can change your sense-of-self and everything you know for a few short hours.

The effects take about half an hour, to an hour, to kick in, and they last for between five and seven hours. Some people enjoy psychedelic art surrounding them in the background, appreciate nice music, and some people like to just sit and chat, stare, reflect or share the experience together.

Some people record their experiences, writing or drawing things that come to mind, as the effects of psychedelic drugs have been known to induce creativity. You can read about peoples tripping journeys online.

Mushrooms are mind-altering, so people generally report on the importance of tripping in a safe environment. One key element from trip reports people post online is being around people you trust and avoiding situations where they need to make important decisions.

. . .

Losing yourself for a bit?

Ever heard of an out-of-body experience? Or felt a detachment from your sense of self, or like you were floating above your own body? At times, as humans, we can experience a sort of 'epiphany moment' when we suddenly see things outside of normal realms; behaviors and the feelings which dictate our actions can suddenly transform and we see things in a new way. What can happen with magic mushrooms is that they form temporary new connections between brain cells, making your brain function in different ways. Your thinking can be out of the ordinary, and being on mushrooms may induce these feelings that your brain can also attain naturally.

Our sense-of-self, or who we are, is predicated upon the identity we have crafted for ourselves. This is often based upon our experiences, life events, our personality and those around us. The way we see the world is through our own perspective; it is anchored in the 'ego' or the 'self'. Certain spiritualists are capable of dissolving their ego, and mushrooms can produce similar effects for some. Essentially, they can dissolve all we know to be real; our perception of reality and our sense or perception of self.

We now look at three different people's experiences of real people, and real experiences with nothing left out.

7

OBSERVING A TRIP: TRIP REPORTS

Sometimes the best wisdom comes from experience. But you don't need to experience it yourself to hear about it. We have summarised some trip reports from people who have documented their experiences through journaling. We have selected a few: those that are good, something in between and one that was a negative experiences.

We also took a pick of experiences that happened on varied doses, from 3.5 grams dried, to 10 grams fresh. Like people, every mushroom is different, and every trip varies from person-to-person. One running theme throughout is that mushrooms only work with what you already have. If you are in a bad place, a depressed or anxious state, they can lead to bad experiences, delusions, flashbacks or paranoia.

Someone who is generally well grounded and feeling positive will be more likely to have a more positive experience. If you are feeling rough or anxious, or convince yourself you won't have a good time, or go into the experience with anxiety, it is very likely that with mushrooms this will happen. If you think about it logically, mushrooms take you inward. If you feel ready to explore what's inside, the psychedelic experience could be an interesting one.

Mushrooms can create interesting visuals and distort reality in a physical, visual, way. Interestingly, none of our trip reports speak of visual alterations, rather, they emphasise the way people feel. Starting with a positive experience, this next section walks you through the ups and downs of tripping to give you some real insight.

Trip report one: A positive experience

This is about a spiritual journey from someone who is ready to face their inner-self and others with love.

From the 18th July 2018, an experienced mushroom taker (although he states it had been a while), took a dose of 3.5 grams and wrote about his experience from start to finish.

The author of "positive experience", workdoodler, had the house to himself after his wife and new baby had left for the weekend. The purpose of shrooms for him was a spiritual journey, and one of discovery. The intent of the drug taking seems to influence very much its outcome too.

As you will see throughout, this trip was largely positive, in contrast to the experience further on. Anxiety is common, so it is down to each person to know whether they are likely to be able to handle it or not. While he reports of a positive trip, like many trip journals, this one also reports of facing anxieties mid-way through. This journaler says he is sitting there, midtrip, "about to face MYSELF, MY ANXIETY". He has the mental elasticity to bring himself around though, oscillating back to "letting the negative go and the love overflow".

Trips often go in stages, with the mental state of the person tripping changing, and going in ebbs and flows. After the initial euphoria for this guy, the following part of the trip involved a large amount of introspective activity, internalizing, and caught up in thoughts. For some people, this is a positive and healthy experience. This guy stopped journaling for a time before coming back to his journal after an hour or so in his own thoughts, doing nothing. For the author of this trip report, mushrooms were spiritual and helped him realize a few things (at least at the time). He wrote:

"Through eating shrooms, I was looking for a 'spiritual journey', and I now realize that our lives ARE the spiritual journeys!". Breaking from ordinary thought patterns, mushrooms can have the effect of what is called "altering consciousness."

After various revelations about life and human nature, he went inward again, stopped journaling, and began doodling. Some revelations were more pertinent than others. He writes: "Always keep a RED pen on you! AND plenty of pens to share with fellow human beings". Unlike many other trip reports, this guy journals at the time, thus logging the different stages. Other reports were written retrospectively, but this is largely because they were relatively turbulent at the time.

Trip report two: riding the waves

This one is about the ups and downs of tripping through unexpected events.

This journaler too took 2.5 grams and experienced "unintended" consequences, making the point that, even if you are in a good place emotionally and mentally, things may occur while you are on magic mushrooms that can potentially induce some anxieties. His message is not to refrain from taking magic mushrooms, but to be prepared to "ride the waves", which is the title of his account on shroomery.org.

Unlike idealistic depictions in films or through popular culture, which can at times glamorize drugs, real experiences highlight the good and the bad, letting you make up your own mind. As journaler two shows, mushrooms confront the realities of the depths of your mind and the real world. After planning to trip and go straight to a dubstep gig, this journaler and his friend ended up downtown, tripping in a public place when their gig was canceled. Further still, in their "fragile states of mind" they ended up in a car collision. These guys kept their cool (just about) and concluded that:

"The trip could have gone seriously bad, in fact, it did for a short while, but as mush always does, it taught me something. From that point on I never take psychedelics for the visuals or the "high". I take them to ride out wherever it takes me and my unsuspecting mind. I don't fight the negative thoughts anymore, now I listen to them to see why they are there. Now explaining tripping to someone, visuals are the last thing I mention, not the first. Psychs can be so much more than what most people perceive them as. You just have to ride the waves and land ashore wherever they may take you."[8]

Trip report three: 'anxiety and mushrooms'

This journaler's trip triggered an anxiety attack and ongoing anxiety issues. It offers advice to see a psychologist or to know yourself before tripping.

This person published because they wanted to share their experience with people who have anxieties before taking psychedelics. They were nervous about having a bad trip but took "only ten grams fresh", they wrote. On the first trip, they had "insights and good thoughts for the last two hours", where they "spent most of it throwing a tennis ball at a wall and feeling good about it :)."

Their second trip led to a five-hour anxiety attack in wave after "wave of terror." This report highlighted some issues that resided with this person for five months afterwards: an anxiety disorder they had to seek psychiatric help for. While this person does not blame the mushrooms for the anxiety disorder, they do determine them as a trigger for it. This person, through their experience, offers the following advice:

"Personally, I would advise anyone before taking mushrooms to go visit a psychologist for a few sessions before and make sure you are not suffering from any pre-existing mental conditions. As an analogy, before supercharging your car make sure the engine is ok or it might blow up…"[9]

8

TRIP SITTING, TRIPPING SAFE AND MANAGING A BAD TRIP OR TRIPPER

We know mushrooms are illegal but it is worth knowing what to do, step-by-step if you have a bad trip or come across someone who is. Or maybe you have been picked to be a 'trip-sitter', a sound and measured sober friend who does not judge and keeps friends out of danger and in a happy, safe, space.

If you are having a bad trip:

1. Take deep breaths. Say: "it will pass, it will pass".

2. Close your eyes tightly and open them again.

3. Go and put some chill music on.

4. Have a nice cartoon cued up and ready to watch.

5. Distract yourself.

6. Get some fresh air (no where dangerous).

7. Take vitamin C or have a sugary drink.

. . .

If someone you know is having a bad trip, or you are trip sitting and someone reaches out:

1. Take them seriously but do not freak out. Listen and tell them to redirect their focus on something nice (it helps if you know the sort of things that are pleasant to experience whilst on mushrooms).

2. Put on some nice music (nothing too distorted, heavy or intense).

3. Don't give them any other drugs or anything. Do not encourage them to take more mushrooms.

4. Get some fresh air but stay safe.

5. If they are near an open window or anything else unsafe, remove them from danger and bring them back to safety, calmly telling them: "it will pass, time is moving on and this will all pass, I am here".

6. If they continue to behave in an unsafe way, or move towards traffic, or attempt to harm themselves and others, do not hesitate to call an ambulance or emergency services. Do not panic and know that mushrooms as a substance generally do not kill people and this is likely a panic attack that will pass.

9
WHAT DO THE RESEARCHERS SAY ABOUT THE EXPERIENCE?

The trip reports or case studies we looked at generally coincide with the academic literature. Research participants generally experienced the same cycles in changes of emotion, consciousness and perception over the course of four to six hours. Medium doses tend to lead to internalization or introspection, euphoria or dream-like states, synaesthesia and adjust perceptions of time and space.

Attention spans can be altered and the research states, like the trip reports above, there are oscillations from pleasant through to panic and dysphoric. Interestingly, the research also indicates that interpersonal support in a setting can reduce panic and increase positive experiences. In other words, tripping alone can be a dangerous business.

If you are going to take them, trip aware: know yourself and your surroundings. See our Do's and Don't section for safer tripping.

There has been some revised research into the controlled testing of the active properties of mushrooms and their potential benefits to jolt people out of addiction or mental health issues. The next section explores this. However, this next part should be read as rather separate to the recreational use of uncontrolled amounts of a drug in a domestic or social environment.

10

MUSHROOMS AND MENTAL HEALTH

The experiences of people on magic mushrooms, or tales of people 'going mad' after toxic doses, lead to a bit of a confusing picture. That is, if you throw the research about the potential benefits magic mushrooms have on mental health into the mix, you might see the two ideas as totally contradictory. Let's say, at this point, that there is a massive difference between drugs research in a controlled environment and buying something on the street from a person you don't know and taking them with friends.

Dr Philip Gerans, author of *The Measure of Madness: Philosophy of Mind, Cognitive Neuroscience, and Delusional Thought* (2014) and Chris Lethby who explores psychedelic drugs from a philosopher's point of view, recently teamed together to explore the way in which psychedelic drugs may have an impact on mental health disorders. [10]

This is the kind of research that can be extracted and misinterpreted as powerful sound bites that advocate the use of uncontrolled substances for mental health disorders. People should also be aware of the powerful warnings *against* using these drugs in an uncontrolled way to manage mental health disorders or anything similar. In fact, it is unwise to self-medicate, and experts actually warn against taking hallucinogens if you have a history of psychosis or other serious conditions, as our case studies above did demonstrate.

The following extract is about this study which simply looked at a controlled way that aspects of the drug's active properties may be used for positive gain. Headlines like this: "Active Ingredient in Shrooms Could 'Reset' Brains of Depressed People" from the subsection of Vice, certainly catch people's attention, but could be misleading without more context.

The basic premise in Geran's and Lethby's research is that psychedelic drugs like psilocybin mushrooms are transformative, and thus can provide a shock to the system, essentially rewiring the brain and assisting people with addiction or depression. While everyone experiences the world differently, we do so based upon patterns and models of the brain. The idea is that mushrooms can help to break these patterns of behavior and challenge the model to which we are bound. For example, if we are conditioned to be distrusting of others, the argument is psychedelic therapy could break these patterns.

A study from New York University also tested psilocybin-assisted therapy in a clinical trial. Researchers also interviewed thirteen adults who had previously taken part in a study.[11] Patients who reported anxiety at the start of the experience, all described a transformation in interpersonal relationships, and some felt a new connection with other humans and the rest of the world.

Seemingly, this is nothing new and has been experienced by many people taking mushrooms. The researchers of this study pointed out that very little had been done to explore the individual (subjective) experience of magic mushrooms and they believe that a combination of psilocybin along with psychotherapy could alleviate anxiety disorders.

Figure 7. A psilocybin study session at John Hopkins. (Wikimedia)

However, for every argument for the potential benefits of this, there are many other counter-arguments. Generally speaking, as testified to in the trip reports you can find online, people with good mental health enjoy positive trips. Those with underlying anxieties should avoid psychedelic experiences altogether. And mushrooms and their doses of psilocybin, and the effects they have on mental health are unpredictable and uncontrolled. Researchers point out that testing drugs in a controlled way is not an endorsement for their recreational use but, maybe the Mexican healer Maria Sabina was onto something back in the 1950s.

11

FREQUENTLY ASKED QUESTIONS

These are all your frequently asked questions, at a glance.

Some of you might want a quick overview of mushrooms and tripping. While we in no way promote the use of illegal drugs, we all
have a responsibility to know the facts.

Are mushrooms addictive?

No, mushrooms are generally not recorded as being addictive.
Tolerance for mushrooms builds up after repeated usage so, generally speaking, mushrooms do not encourage repeated use in a short
space of time. There is always the chance that you become addicted
to the experience of tripping, taking mushrooms, or experimenting
with them.

Some people develop a lifelong fascination with them, growing them
or becoming experts on various strains, types and experiences.
There are people who have made a career from this or have become
expert bloggers, writers or scientists on the topic.

. . .

Are there drugs tests for magic mushrooms?

Psilocybin, the active properties in magic mushrooms, turns into psilocin. This can be found in urine and hair samples. Traces of magic mushrooms disappear pretty quickly. In urine, it is normally gone within a few hours, maximum 24 or, in cases of chronic doses or overuse, 48 hours. It can remain in your blood for 1-2 days but normally disappears pretty quickly compared to other substances.

How do magic mushrooms affect the brain?

Magic mushrooms affect the brain through the chemical compounds attaching themselves to serotonin (happy) receptors in the brain. They alter consciousness by disrupting thought patterns and changing the normal signal patterns around your brain, meaning that you perceive reality in a different way, often processing visual and sensory information in new ways.

Can magic mushrooms be spiked or laced?

Because of their appearance, they are unlikely to be cut with other drugs. However, some reports have suggested that normal mushrooms have been sold to unsuspecting people and that some of these are laced with LSD instead of organically containing the psychoactive properties of mushrooms, psilocybin. Also, if they are crushed and dried/in pill form, you will not know what is inside or whether they are cut with something else.

How long does a trip last?

A trip generally lasts between four to six hours when the mushrooms are eaten. It takes between thirty to sixty minutes to come up.

What do magic mushrooms look like?

With over 180 psilocybin containing mushroom species out there, it is impossible to summarise what magic mushrooms look like specifically. However, what they have in common is that they have a cap and a stem and gills underneath. Their color varies considerably. Many of them are very easily confused with poisonous varieties and spore prints have to be taken in order to identify them correctly.

How do magic mushrooms make you feel?

Magic mushrooms have an effect on the central nervous system. How they make you feel is very much dependent on you. They can induce euphoria-like feelings, visual sensations, an altered sense of time and space but also, in some cases, anxiety or nervousness.

Are magic mushrooms dangerous?

Magic mushrooms are generally considered 'safe' in chemical terms. Their danger lies in triggering psychotic episodes if you have mental health disorders. In very rare cases they can cause prolonged anxiety. They generally do not result in death unless dangerous activity is carried out whilst under the influence. They are not as known to cause flashbacks (as in the case of LSD).

How are mushrooms stored?

Once picked, mushrooms remain fresh from between five and ten days, depending entirely on their water content. You can store them in the fridge. However, like any living organism, they can rot if left longer. If not, you can put them into a container or sealed bag and freeze them for around seven months to one year. Many people choose to dry them for use much later on. This is most people's preferred option. Psilocybin mushroom potency is reduced through drying but not by a significant amount at all.

.   .   .

How do you dry mushrooms?

Drying them can be achieved by letting them air dry on a piece of paper or speeding up the process by drying them on a piece of paper on a radiator. After you have dried them, it is best to put them in an airtight container, although you should be aware that their strength will gradually decrease over time. You can also put them in an oven with the door open or in an oven with the door closed (as long as the temperature does not go over 95 Fahrenheit/ 36 degrees).

How do you prepare magic mushrooms?

This is entirely up to the person taking them but most people prefer tea as it is gentler on the stomach. Be careful not to boil the water but to just stew the mushrooms in warm water. You can add herbs, flavorings or herbal tea to improve on the taste. When mushrooms are picked fresh, they should be rinsed before consumption.

Can you eat mushrooms as they are?

Mushrooms are also eaten fresh or dried, however, this can cause stomach cramps and vomiting, and the taste is unpleasant, so most people prefer to brew tea.

How many magic mushrooms do you need to trip?

This is varied depending on the type/strain.

Liberty Caps dried require one to three grams for a medium dose, and three to seven for a strong dose, or two to eighteen fresh for a moderate trip and seven to forty two fresh for a strong one. *Cubensis* require one to three dried, or two to seven for a stronger trip. For *cubensis* that are fresh, the maximum dose for a very strong trip is up to twenty eight grams fresh. These are very rough guidelines.

· · ·

What is it like to trip?

Tripping can be euphoric, visual and cause altered consciousness. Throughout the duration, you may oscillate between happy feelings, panicky, relaxed, insular, thoughtful and creative.

Should you take other drugs with mushrooms?

It is inadvisable to take other drugs with magic mushrooms. Some people take cannabis alongside it which they say can reduce sickness at the start for the first hour. However, cannabis can also increase anxiety and panic which could combine with the mushrooms. There are reports online of people going overboard and being pulled in many different directions by a cocktail of substances. Amphetamines (speed) and cocaine are especially to be avoided. They just don't go. We discuss this in more detail on the mixology section in this guide.

What do mushrooms do to the brain?

After the psilocybin is converted to psilocin in the body, it is pumped to the brain where it increases a type of serotonin (5HT-2A) – which controls the neural transmission of things affecting mood, perception, memory, awareness and appetite.

What are the after effects? (Comedowns)

After effects of mushrooms, comedowns, are not really a major feature of the drug. As we saw with trip report 3, some people experience psychological effects triggered by the mushrooms themselves, but there is nothing necessarily chemical that occurs. The day after taking mushrooms, people can generally feel tired or a little confused, or things and experiences that have occurred during the tripping itself can stay with you (good or bad). Comedowns as to the sort felt on ecstasy or MDMA are not as comparable.

12

BONUS CHAPTER: DO'S AND DON'TS

Here is our list of shrooming do's and don'ts. First and foremost make sure you know the legal guidelines of the country you're in ton taking magic mushrooms.

.

DO sort out your environment:

You are way more likely to have an enjoyable experience if you are in a good space.

1. Advice from seasoned trippers: clean the flat, house or room you are tripping in. You will find that dirtiness looks worse than ever, and even clean things will still look a little bit distorted and gross.
2. Make yourself a comfortable spot and keep things a nice temperature. The journey is supposed to be for your mind, you don't want to feel cold and edgy.

DON'T have any freaky posters around. If it freaks you out when you are sober, it will freak you out ten-fold if you take magic mushrooms

DO take a small dose to start with. Users say to take small amounts to see where you get on. Once they kick into your system, you can't remove them. We've gone through already how these organic drugs are an absolute lottery when it comes to dosage.

DO relax and go with it. Trip reporter number three tried to make herself sick to get rid of the effects but she had to ride out the trip for another four hours. Trip reporter number two said to be aware and ride the waves. Try your best to relax. Make sure you have the capacity to face your *known* anxieties and have the ability to calm yourself down *before* you even consider tripping, a bit like trip reporter number one.

DO listen to nice music. Queue up your playlist and avoid nasty surprises. Users have also noted that you might not even notice if the music has been off for a while!

DO enjoy the sun and fresh air in a safe environment.

DO get into a brilliant headspace before taking them. Mushrooms and bad trips can kind of work on a self-fulfilling prophecy basis.

DO write and journal to share your experiences.

DO NOT TAKE THEM IF:

. . .

You are naturally anxious and prone to panic attacks (or haven't had one before but think you could). Mushrooms are completely inadvisable. Why would you go somewhere that scares you? That is the trip you will have.

You or your family have a history of psychosis, paranoia or mental illness

Your friends convince you of it. This is a personal choice. Messing about with drugs is not cool when it goes completely wrong and you are left downtown with three people freaking out staring at their hands and unable to get into a cab.

You're in crappy company. If you are with someone who makes you feel uncomfortable, or edgy, or is generally a bit unsupportive, wait for another time altogether and do it with people who love you.

You are super young. You don't want to be messing with your brain while you are still growing and have a concoction of hormones going about. Just wait until you know yourself and feel comfortable in your own skin.

You are high already. Panic and paranoia strike fast...why mess with that mix?

Other Tips

DO stay informed. Read, read, read! There are tons of trip reports online. Avoid the fake and glamorized blogs, and go for the real, raw, unedited, versions

. . .

DO make good decisions about where to trip before you start. If you start off indoors, you are likely to stay safe. While there are no real incidents of deaths *because* of the substance in mushrooms, there are tons of reports out there about excessive and toxic doses (hard to regulate) leading to death, criminal activity and all sorts of horrors.

DON'T go picking random mushrooms. You **don't know** what you're doing, and a small change in gill spacing, stem size or an invisible change in spore print, can result in death.

DON'T break the law. You can go on mushroom retreats to countries where the law is more relaxed.

DO look after your fellow trippers.

DO get a trip sitter, a sober person who will look after you.

DO love yourself and others, no matter what.

AFTERWORD

Hopefully, you have enjoyed this explorer's guide, and it has met your curiosity for information on magic mushrooms.

We definitely journeyed through time and explored the human relationship with magic mushrooms. We saw trip reports from 9000 years ago on a cave wall and the first viral trip report that sparked the whole hippie movement towards hallucinogens.

We took a tour of mushroom prep, dangers, and benefits of magic mushrooms according to some pretty radical research in the making.

We shared three diverse experiences and invite you to share and read more. Attached are resources if you'd like to do some further readings and want to discover more about this fascinating drug.

ALSO BY ALEX GIBBONS

Did you enjoy the book or learn something new? It really helps out small publishers like Alex if you could leave a quick review on Amazon so others in the community can also find the book!

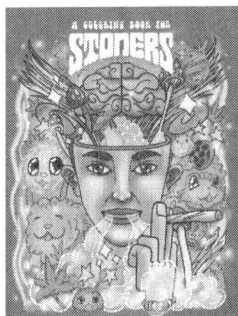

⭐ ⭐ ⭐ ⭐ ⭐

———

Want to chill and experience the benefits of mindfulness? Want to do something productive while watching random videos on YouTube?

Get this fun stoner themed coloring book to scribble on for your next trip. Search for 'Alex Gibbons Stoner Coloring Book' on Amazon to get yours now!

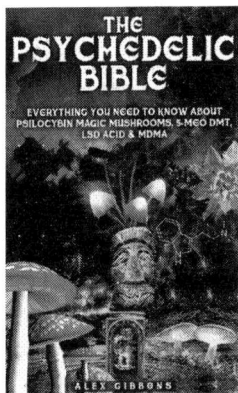

———

Thinking about taking other magical drugs? Ever wondered what exactly happens when you take them? Want to make sure you don't have a bad trip?

If you want to read more about the history, origins and effects of Magic Mushrooms, LSD/Acid or DMT, search for 'The Psychedelic Bible' on Amazon!

For daily posts on all things Psychedelic, follow us on Instagram @Psychedelic.curiosity

Manufactured by Amazon.ca
Bolton, ON

14803600R00035